1

CW00797426

by Iain Gray

Lang**Syne**

PUBLISHING

WRITING *to* REMEMBER

79 Main Street, Newtongrange,
Midlothian EH22 4NA
Tel: 0131 344 0414   Fax: 0845 075 6085
E-mail: info@lang-syne.co.uk
www.langsyneshop.co.uk

Design by Dorothy Meikle
Printed by Printwell Ltd
© Lang Syne Publishers Ltd 2016

ISBN 978-1-85217-477-4

Tait

MOTTO:
Always the same
(and)
Think and thank.

CREST:
A blue lion inset with a silver cross
(and)
An arm with the hand holding a pine branch.

TERRITORY:
The Borders.

NAME variations include:
Tate
Taite
Tayt

Echoes of a far distant past
can still be found in most names

Chapter one:

Origins of Scottish surnames

by George Forbes

It all began with the Normans.

For it was they who introduced surnames into common usage more than a thousand years ago, initially based on the title of their estates, local villages and chateaux in France to distinguish and identify these landholdings, usually acquired at the point of a bloodstained sword.

Such grand descriptions also helped enhance the prestige of these arrogant warlords and generally glorify their lofty positions high above the humble serfs slaving away below in the pecking order who only had single names, often with Biblical connotations as in Pierre and Jacques.

The only descriptive distinctions among this peasantry concerned their occupations, like Pierre the swineherd or Jacques the ferryman.

The Normans themselves were originally Vikings (or Northmen) who raided, colonised and eventually settled down around the French coastline.

They had sailed up the Seine in their longboats in 900 AD under their ferocious leader Rollo and ruled the roost in north east France before sailing over to conquer England, bringing their relatively new tradition of having surnames with them.

It took another hundred years for the Normans to percolate northwards and surnames did not begin to appear in Scotland until the thirteenth century.

These adventurous knights brought an aura of chivalry with them and it was said no damsel of any distinction would marry a man unless he had at least two names.

The family names included that of Scotland's great hero Robert De Brus and his compatriots were warriors from families like the De Morevils, De Umphravils, De Berkelais, De Quincis, De Viponts and De Vaux.

As the knights settled the boundaries of their vast estates, they took territorial names, as in Hamilton, Moray, Crawford, Cunningham, Dunbar, Ross, Wemyss, Dundas, Galloway, Renfrew, Greenhill, Hazelwood, Sandylands and Church-hill.

Other names, though not with any obvious geographical or topographical features, nevertheless derived from ancient parishes like Douglas, Forbes, Dalyell and Guthrie.

Other surnames were coined in connection with occupations, castles or legendary deeds. Stuart originated in the word steward, a prestigious post which was an integral part of any large medieval household. The same applied to Cooks, Chamberlains, Constables and Porters.

Borders towns and forts – needed in areas like the Debateable Lands which were constantly fought over by feuding local families – had their own distinctive names; and it was often from them that the resident groups took their communal titles, as in the Grahams of Annandale, the Elliots and Armstrongs of the East Marches, the Scotts and Kerrs of Teviotdale and Eskdale.

Even physical attributes crept into surnames, as in Small, Little and More (the latter being 'beg' in Gaelic), Long or Lang, Stark, Stout, Strong or Strang and even Jolly.

Mieklejohns would have had the strength of several men, while Littlejohn was named after the legendary sidekick of Robin Hood.

Colours got into the act with Black, White, Grey, Brown and Green (Red developed into Reid,

Ruddy or Ruddiman). Blue was rare and nobody ever wanted to be associated with yellow.

Pompous worthies took the name Wiseman, Goodman and Goodall.

Words intimating the sons of leading figures were soon affiliated into the language as in Johnson, Adamson, Richardson and Thomson, while the Norman equivalent of Fitz (from the French-Latin 'filius' meaning 'son') cropped up in Fitzmaurice and Fitzgerald.

The prefix 'Mac' was 'son of' in Gaelic and clans often originated with occupations – as in MacNab being sons of the Abbot, MacPherson and MacVicar being sons of the minister and MacIntosh being sons of the chief.

The church's influence could be found in the names Kirk, Clerk, Clarke, Bishop, Friar and Monk. Proctor came from a church official, Singer and Sangster from choristers, Gilchrist and Gillies from Christ's servant, Mitchell, Gilmory and Gilmour from servants of St Michael and Mary, Malcolm from a servant of Columba and Gillespie from a bishop's servant.

The rudimentary medical profession was represented by Barber (a trade which also once included dentistry and surgery) as well as Leech or Leitch.

Businessmen produced Merchants, Mercers, Monypennies, Chapmans, Sellers and Scales, while down at the old village watermill the names that cropped up included Miller, Walker and Fuller.

Other self explanatory trades included Coopers, Brands, Barkers, Tanners, Skinners, Brewsters and Brewers, Tailors, Saddlers, Wrights, Cartwrights, Smiths, Harpers, Joiners, Sawyers, Masons and Plumbers.

Even the scenery was utilised as in Craig, Moor, Hill, Glen, Wood and Forrest.

Rank, whether high or low, took its place with Laird, Barron, Knight, Tennant, Farmer, Husband, Granger, Grieve, Shepherd, Shearer and Fletcher.

The hunt and the chase supplied Hunter, Falconer, Fowler, Fox, Forrester, Archer and Spearman.

The renowned medieval historian Froissart, who eulogised about the romantic deeds of chivalry (and who condemned Scotland as being a poverty stricken wasteland), once sniffily dismissed the peasantry of his native France as the jacquerie (or the jacques-without-names) but it was these same humble folk who ended up overthrowing the arrogant aristocracy.

In the olden days, only the blueblooded knights of antiquity were entitled to full, proper names, both Christian and surnames, but with the passing of time and a more egalitarian, less feudal atmosphere, more respectful and worthy titles spread throughout the populace as a whole.

Echoes of a far distant past can still be found in most names and they can be borne with pride in commemoration of past generations who fought and toiled in some capacity or other to make our nation what it now is, for good or ill.

Chapter two:

Wars of Independence

Derived from the Old Norse tietr, meaning 'glad' or 'cheerful', 'Tait' and its equally popular spelling variant of 'Tate' has been present on British shores from earliest times.

An Uluric Tates is recorded in the present-day English county of Suffolk in 1095, while the Old English given name of 'Tata' lends itself to the names of a number of English villages that include Tatsfield and Tatterhill.

It is from a 'Tait' family settled in Suffolk at an early date that one of the family mottoes of *Think and thank* and crest of an arm with the hand holding a pine branch derive.

In Ireland, particularly in the ancient northern province of Ulster, the name first began to appear in large numbers in the seventeenth century, while a John Tayt is recorded in Montrose, in the northeast of Scotland, in the early 1360s.

An indication of the geographical spread of the name throughout Scotland is that an Alexander Tayt is recorded in Edinburgh in 1381, an Adam Tayt in Paisley in 1432, a Christie Tett and Dand Taitt in Kelso, in the Borders, in 1567, while it is also recorded much further north, in Orkney, in 1575.

Despite the wide distribution of the name, it was the Borders that for centuries was the main stamping ground of the Taits – with one of the first established families of the name being the Taits of Pirn, in Tweeddale.

It was in the Borders that the Taits found themselves in the first line of defence from English invasion.

Scotland had been thrown into crisis in 1285 with the death of Alexander II and the death four years later of his successor, the Maid of Norway, who died while en route to Scotland to take up the crown.

John Balliol was enthroned at Scone as King of Scots in 1292 – but fatefully for the nation the ambitious Edward I of England was invited to arbitrate in the bitter dispute over the succession to the throne, and the hapless Balliol was Edward's chosen man.

The Scots rose in revolt against the imperialist designs of the English king in July of 1296 but, living up to his reputation of 'Hammer of the Scots', he brought the entire nation under his subjugation little less than a month later, garrisoning strategic locations throughout the country.

To reinforce his domination of the nation, 1,500 earls, bishops, burgesses and other landowners were required to sign a humiliating treaty of fealty known as the *Ragman Roll*, because of the number of ribbons that dangled from the seals of the reluctant signatories.

The great freedom fighter William Wallace raised the banner of revolt against the English occupation of Scotland in May of 1297, after slaying Sir William Heselrig, Sheriff of Lanark, in revenge for the killing of his young wife, Marion.

Proving an expert in the tactics of guerrilla warfare, Wallace and his hardened band of freedom fighters inflicted stunning defeats on the English garrisons – and one of their near impenetrable hiding places was the inhospitable depths of Ettrick Forest, in the Borders.

It was here that Wallace was joined by many battle-hardened Border fighters, including bearers of the Tait name.

Wallace's revolt spread like wildfire, culminating in the liberation of practically all of Scotland following the battle of Stirling Bridge, on September 11, 1297.

While Wallace had raised the south of Scotland in revolt, his equally able commander Sir

Andrew Murray, who along with his father had been captured at the battle of Dunbar about a year earlier, had sparked off a rising in the northeast.

The bold Murray managed to escape from his confinement in Chester Castle and, returning to his homelands and raising a force of loyal kinsmen and others who suffered under English occupation, captured the English held castles of Banff, Elgin, Inverness and Urquhart.

The forces of Wallace and Murray met up and prepared to meet a mighty English invasion force that had been hurriedly despatched north by Edward I.

Despite having only 36 cavalry and 8,000 foot soldiers, compared to an army under the Earl of Surrey that boasted no less than 200 knights and 10,000 foot soldiers, the Scots held a strategic advantage that they exploited to the full.

Positioning their forces on the heights of the Abbey Craig, on the outskirts of Stirling, and where the imposing Wallace Monument now stands, Wallace and Murray waited patiently as Essex's force slowly made its way across a narrow wooden bridge that spanned the waters of the Forth.

As the bulk of the English army crossed onto the marshy ground at the foot of the Abbey Craig, the piercing blast of a hunting horn signalled a ferocious charge down the hillside of massed ranks of Scottish spearmen.

Trapped on the boggy ground, the English were incapable of putting up any effective resistance.

They were hacked to death in their hundreds, while many others drowned in the fast-flowing waters of the Forth in their heavy armour as they attempted to make their way back across the narrow bridge.

Defeated at the battle of Falkirk on July 22, 1298, after earlier being appointed Guardian of Scotland in a solemn ceremony that had taken place in the depths of Ettrick Forest, Wallace was eventually betrayed and captured in August of 1305.

On the black day for Scotland of August 23 of that year, he was brutally executed in London on the orders of a vengeful Edward I.

Nearly nine years later, in June of 1314, a 20,000-strong English army under Edward's successor, Edward II, was defeated by a Scots army less than half this strength commanded by the great warrior king Robert the Bruce.

In the ranks of his army were not only Highlanders and Islanders but also a sizeable contingent of Lowlanders who included Borderers such as the Taits.

Ironically, it was a through a misguided sense of chivalry that the battle occurred in the first place.

By midsummer of 1313 the mighty fortress of Stirling Castle was occupied by an English garrison under the command of Sir Philip Mowbray.

Bruce's brother, Edward, agreed to a pledge by Mowbray that if the castle was not relieved by battle by midsummer of the following year, then he would surrender. This made battle inevitable, and by June 23 of 1314 the two armies faced one another at Bannockburn, in sight of the castle.

It was on this day that Bruce slew the English knight Sir Henry de Bohun in single combat, but the battle proper was not fought until the following day, shortly after the rise of the midsummer sun.

The English cavalry launched a desperate but futile charge on the densely packed ranks of Scottish spearmen known as schiltrons.

By the time the sun had sank slowly in the west the English army had been totally routed, with Edward himself only narrowly managing to make his escape from the carnage of the battlefield.

Scotland's independence had been secured, to the glory of Bruce and his loyal army and at terrible cost to the English.

Chapter three:

Life on the borderline

Despite Bruce's great victory at Bannockburn, the bloody Wars of Independence continued, seeing large tracts of the Tait homeland of the Borders laid waste.

This was not only at the hands of the invading armies, but also by the retreating local population in a bid to deny the enemy food, forage and shelter.

The great Border abbeys of Dryburgh, Jedburgh, Kelso and Melrose fell victim to successive waves of English armies.

Founded by David I in 1150 and dedicated to St Mary, Dryburgh Abbey was burnt in 1322, 1385 and 1544, while Jedburgh Abbey, founded by David in about 1138 was attacked in 1297, 1523 and on two occasions between 1544 and 1545.

Kelso Abbey, founded originally at Selkirk in 1113 but moved and built in grander style in Kelso in 1138, was largely destroyed between 1544 and 1545, while Melrose Abbey, founded in about 1136, and in common with Dryburgh, was sacked in 1322, 1385 and 1545.

The poignantly beautiful ruins of these abbeys dominate their local landscapes to this day and are major tourist attractions.

When not engaged in battling English invaders, bearers of the Tait name were still to be found with sword or dagger in hand.

This was as one of the lawless Border families who were frequently to be found 'reiving', or raiding, not only their neighbours' livestock, but also that of their neighbours across the border.

The word 'bereaved', for example, indicating to have suffered loss, derives from the original 'reived', meaning to have suffered loss of property.

A Privy Council report of 1608 graphically described how the 'wild incests, adulteries, convocation of the lieges, shooting and wearing of hackbuts, pistols, lances, daily bloodshed, oppression, and disobedience in civil matters, neither are nor has been punished.'

A constant thorn in the flesh of both the English and Scottish authorities was the cross-border raiding and pillaging carried out by well-mounted and heavily armed men, the contingent from the Scottish side of the border known and feared as 'moss troopers.'

In an attempt to bring order to what was

known as the wild 'debateable land' on both sides of the border, Alexander II of Scotland had in 1237 signed the Treaty of York, which for the first time established the Scottish border with England as a line running from the Solway to the Tweed.

On either side of the border there were three 'marches' or areas of administration, the West, East and Middle Marches, and a warden governed these.

Complaints from either side of the border were dealt with on Truce Days, when the wardens of the different marches would act as arbitrators.

There was also a law known as the Hot Trod, that granted anyone who had their livestock stolen the right to pursue the thieves and recover their property.

The post of March Warden was a powerful and lucrative one, with rival families vying for the position – and the marches became virtually a law unto themselves.

In the Scottish borderlands, the Homes and Swintons dominated the East March, while the Armstrongs, Maxwells, Johnstones and Grahams were the rulers of the West March.

The Taits, along with others who included the Douglases, Gilchrists, Rutherfords and Turnbulls held sway in the Middle March.

It was following the Union of the Crowns in 1603 that James I (James VI of Scotland) attempted to crush the Border mayhem once and for all.

The very term 'Borders' was abolished and renamed 'the Middle Shires', while scores of particularly unruly families were forcibly uprooted and either conscripted into military service or banished to Ireland.

Other, more law-abiding, families found themselves in Ireland through the early seventeenth century policy of 'Plantation' – the settling of loyal subjects on land previously held by what were deemed to be 'rebellious' native Irish.

Descendants of many of these Scots-Irish, including bearers of the Tait and Tate names, later found new lives for themselves in foreign parts, particularly North America, Australia and New Zealand, and this is where many of the name are to be found in large numbers today.

One noteworthy nineteenth century bearer of the Tait name was Archibald Campbell Tait who, unusually for a Scot, not only became a priest in the Church of England but also an Archbishop of Canterbury.

Born in Edinburgh in 1811, he converted

from the Presbyterian faith of his parents to the Scottish Episcopal faith and was later confirmed in the Church of England while a student at Oxford University.

A senior tutor at the university at the age of only 26, he later held the post for a time as headmaster of Rugby School, where one of his pupils was the future literary figure Lewis Carroll, author of *Alice in Wonderland*.

Leaving the world of education to follow his religious vocation, he was appointed to the Church of England deanery of Carlisle in 1849, while he was consecrated Bishop of London seven years later.

Refusing the Archbishopric of York in 1862, he was enthroned as Archbishop of Canterbury in 1868, serving with distinction as such until his death in 1882.

Another noted nineteenth century bearer of the name is one whose legacy survives to this day not only through the multi-national business Tate and Lyle but also through the renowned art institution known as The Tate.

This was Henry Tate, the English sugar merchant and philanthropist born in 1819 near Chorley, Lancashire.

The son of a clergyman, he was aged 13 when apprenticed as a grocer in Liverpool.

Only seven years later, through having carefully saved his meagre earnings and by dint of hard work, he was able to set up his own grocery shop; by the time he was aged 35, this had grown to a chain of six stores, while in 1859 he entered into partnership with the sugar refiners John Wright and Co.

Gaining overall control of the company ten years later and having already sold his grocery business, Tate renamed the sugar refining company Henry Tate and Sons.

Buying a German patent for a method of making sugar cubes, he built a new refinery in Liverpool and, in 1877, opened the Silvertown refinery in London, which remains in production to this day.

Rapidly accumulating vast wealth, Tate was also concerned for the welfare of his workers and became a generous benefactor of a number of charitable concerns.

It was in 1889 that he donated his collection of contemporary paintings to the nation, also donating £80,000 towards the construction of a gallery to house the collection and other works to be added in the future.

The gallery opened in London in 1897 as the National Gallery of British Art, later named the Tate Gallery in his honour.

Now known as The Tate, it is a network of four art museums – the Tate Modern, London, Tate Britain, also in London, Tate Liverpool and Tate St Ives, in Cornwall – which house the United Kingdom's National Collection of British Art and International and Contemporary Art.

A modest man, Tate had refused the offer of a knighthood on a number of occasions – until finally accepting a year before his death in 1899 after being told the Royal Family would be offended if he refused the honour again.

The multi-national and British-based company of Tate and Lyle was meanwhile formed 22 years after Tate's death through the merger of Henry Tate and Sons with Abram Lyle and Sons.

Returning to the battlefield, where bearers of the Tait name were frequently to be found from earliest times, James Tait, born in Dumfries in 1886, was a Scots-Canadian recipient of the Victoria Cross (VC), the highest award for valour in the face of enemy action for British and Commonwealth forces.

Immigrating to Canada with his family as a

child, he returned to Europe during the First World War as a lieutenant in the 78th (Winnipeg Grenadiers) Battalion, Canadian Expeditionary Force.

He was posthumously awarded the VC for his actions in August of 1918 in Amiens, France, when he single-handedly attacked and silenced an enemy machine-gunner who had already exacted a heavy toll on his comrades.

His action cleared the way for his battalion to advance, but he was killed; his VC is now on display at the Glenbow Museum, Calgary, Alberta.

During the Second World War, and in the air, Group Captain James Tait was the RAF bomber pilot who conducted more than 100 bombing missions.

Born in 1916 in Manchester and commissioned as a pilot three years before the outbreak of the conflict in 1939, he is best known as the leader of the force of 37 Avro Lancaster bombers of 617 Squadron and 9 Squadron on *Operation Paravane-Catechism*.

This was on November 12, 1944, when three direct hits from the bombers managed to sink the mighty German battleship *Tirpitz* west of Tromsø, Norway.

A recipient of the Distinguished Service Order (DSO), he died in 2007.

Chapter four:

On the world stage

From film and sport to science and literature, bearers of the Tait name and its equally popular spelling variant of Tate have gained fame at an international level.

Nominated for a Golden Globe Award for her performance in the 1967 film *Valley of the Dolls* and hailed at the time as one of Hollywood's most promising newcomers, **Sharon Tate** was the American model and actress stabbed to death in her home in August of 1969 by followers of the self-styled hippy leader Charles Manson.

Born in 1943 in Dallas and married to the acclaimed film director Roman Polanski, she had been eight and a half months pregnant when four of Manson's followers, known as the Manson family, broke into her home in Benedict Canyon, Los Angeles.

The actress and her unborn child were killed after she was repeatedly stabbed, while four others were also murdered.

Although not present at the murders, Manson was later convicted for having ordered the killing spree, for reasons that still remain unexplained to this day.

In contemporary times, **Catherine Tate** is the award-winning English actress, comedian and writer best known for television's *The Catherine Tate Show*.

Born in 1968 in Bloomsbury, London and famous for the catch-phrase 'Am I bovvered?', from her show first screened in 2004, she also starred as Doctor Who's companion in the 2008 series of the popular television show.

Also having performed with the Royal Shakespeare Company, her many awards include an International Emmy nomination and seven BAFTA Awards for *The Catherine Tate Show*.

In Australia, **Nick Tate**, born in 1942 in Sydney, is the actor best known for his role of Alan Carter in the 1970s science fiction television series *Space: 1999* and for the role in the 1980s of James Hamilton in the soap *Sons and Daughters*.

Behind the camera lens, **Margaret Tait** was the Scottish filmmaker and poet born in 1918 in Kirkwall, Orkney.

Returning to Scotland after studying film-making in Rome in the early 1950s, she founded Ancona Films and settled in her native Orkney.

Inspired by its landscape and culture, she made a number of short films that include the 1964 *Where I am is Here* and, released a year before her death in 1999, *Garden Pieces*.

Best known as the Australian writer and director of the 1906 *The Story of the Kelly Gang* – the world's first feature length narrative film – **Charles Tait** was born in 1868 in Castlemaine, Victoria.

One of nine children and the son of a tailor from Scalloway, in the Shetland Islands, who had immigrated from Scotland to Australia, Tait and two of his brothers became leading concert, theatrical and film entrepreneurs; he died in 1933.

Bearers of the Tait and Tate names have particularly excelled in the highly competitive world of sport.

Commonwealth champion in 2006 in the 200-metres backstroke and 200-metres individual medley events, **Gregor Tait** is the Scottish swimmer born in 1979 in Glasgow.

In the boxing ring, **Johnny Tate**, born in 1955 in Marion, Arkansas, was the American prize-fighter and Olympic boxer known to his fans as "Big John."

World heavyweight champion from 1979 to

1980, he was also the winner of a bronze medal at the 1976 Olympics in Montreal.

He was killed in a road accident in 1998.

Also in the boxing ring, **Frank Tate**, born in 1964 in Detroit, is the American boxer who was the 1983 Golden Gloves Light Middleweight Champion and a gold-medallist at the 1984 Olympics.

In the rough and tumble that is the game of rugby, **Alan Tait** is the former rugby league and rugby union player who played outside centre for Scotland from 1987 to 1999.

Born in Kelso, in the Tait heartland of the Borders, he played club rugby for the town and also the Newcastle Falcons – with whom he was appointed head coach in 2009.

A member of the silver medal-winning team at the 2007 Commonwealth Games, **Mathew Tait** played club rugby for Leicester Tigers and Newcastle and Sale.

Born in 1986 in Shotley Bridge, Co. Durham, he is a younger brother of the rugby union player **Alex Tait**, born in 1988, and who has played for Newcastle Falcons.

On the cricket pitch, yet another **Alex Tait** is the New Zealand cricketer, born in 1972, who played in five One Day Internationals for his country in the late 1990s.

Also in New Zealand, **Blyth Tait** is the leading equestrian whose many awards include four Olympic medals.

Born in 1961 in Whangarei, she won a silver as part of the three-day event team and a bronze in the individual event in 1992, while in 1996 she won a bronze for the three-day event team and a gold for three-day individual event.

Still in New Zealand, **Robin Tait**, born in 1940 in Dunedin and who died in 1984, was the discus thrower who won the bronze medal in the event at the 1966 Commonwealth Games and gold at the 1974 games.

In the highly cerebral world of chess, **Emory A. Tate, Jr.**, is the American International Master born in 1958 in Chicago.

From chess to the equally cerebral realms of mathematics, **Peter Guthrie Tait** was the Scottish mathematician and physicist known for his 1867 Treatise on Natural Philosophy.

Born in Dalkeith, Midlothian, in 1831, before his death in 1901 he had held a number of academic posts that included professor of mathematics at

Queen's College, Belfast and professor of natural philosophy at Edinburgh University.

Also in the sciences, and back yet again to New Zealand, **Sir Angus Tait** was the electronics innovator and businessman who in 1969 founded what is now Tait Radio Communications – recognised as a world leader in the field of mobile radio.

Born in Oamaru in 1919, he was knighted eight years before his death in 2007, while there is a bronze bust of him outside Christchurch Arts Centre.

Bearers of the Tait name have also made a significant contribution to the world of medicine.

Born in Edinburgh in 1845, **Robert Lawson Tait** was a pioneer of pelvic and abdominal surgery, obstetrics and gynaecology – the treatment that he developed in 1883 for ectopic pregnancy responsible for having saved a countless number of lives to this day.

Considered along with J. Marion Sims as one of the 'fathers of gynaecology' and associated for most of his career with the Birmingham Hospital for Women, he died in 1899.

In the creative world of the written word, no fewer than two of the name have been honoured with the accolade of Poet Laureate.

Born in Dublin in 1652, **Nahum Tate** was the Irish poet, lyricist and hymnist appointed England's Poet Laureate in 1692; he died in 1715.

Across the Atlantic to America, **Allen Tate**, born in 1899 near Winchester, Kentucky, and who died in 1979, was the poet and essayist who was Poet Laureate to the Library of Congress in the early 1940s.

A member of the group known as the Fugitive Poets, his most famous poem is *Ode to the Confederate Dead*.

A member of the American Academy of Arts and letters, **James Tate** is the poet who's *Selected Poems* won a Pulitzer Prize in 1992.

Born in 1953 in Kansas City, Missouri, he also won the National Book Award in 1994 for his poetry collection *Worshipful Company of Fletchers*.

One bearer of the Tait name, much of whose work still graces the landscapes of the world to this day, was the Scottish modernist architect **Thomas Smith Tait**.

Born in Paisley in 1882, the son of a stonemason, he was apprenticed as an architect and also studied at Glasgow School of Art.

Settling in London and working for a time with John Burnett and Partners and later with his own company of Tait and Lorne, he was responsible for the 300ft Tower of Empire that dominated the 1938 Empire Exhibition in Glasgow's Bellahouston Park.

Combining art deco and streamline moderne styles, in 1939 he designed St Andrews House, on the southern flank of Edinburgh's Calton Hill, while he also designed the pylons for the magnificent Sydney Harbour Bridge.

He died in 1954, while other notable architectural works include, in London, the former *Daily Telegraph* offices, Unilever House and Selfridges in Oxford Street.